Bond

10 Minute Tests

11⁺-12⁺ years

Frances Down

Verbal Reasoning

Nelson Thornes

Underline the word in the brackets which goes best with the words given outside the brackets.

Example: word, paragraph, sentence   (pen, cap, <u>letter</u>, top, stop)

1 chat, converse   (read, <u>gossip</u>, lecture, preach, pray)

2 improvise, devise   (invent, plan, <u>prepare</u>, train, examine)

3 succinct, concise   (wordy, rambling, flawed, formal, <u>precise</u>)

4 scandal, shame   (belief, honour, distance, <u>disgrace</u>, worship)

5 guard, shield   (disregard, observe, notice, study, <u>protect</u>)

Underline the two words, one from each group, which are closest in meaning.

Example: (race, shop, <u>start</u>)   (finish, <u>begin</u>, end)

6   (<u>eager</u>, indifferent, content)   (<u>enthusiastic</u>, different, equal)

7   (tribute, celebration, <u>crisis</u>)   (security, <u>danger</u>, dilemma)

8   (rush, <u>charge</u>, toss)   (catch, <u>entrust</u>, turn)

9   (suffer, falter, <u>perish</u>)   (control, master, <u>die</u>)

10 (tease, <u>enrage</u>, encourage)   (<u>infuriate</u>, tickle, magnify)

Underline the word in the brackets closest in meaning to the word in capitals.

Example: UNHAPPY   (unkind   death   laughter   <u>sad</u>   friendly)

11 STALE   (fresh   stark   post   stem   <u>mouldy</u>)

12 ENVY   (<u>jealousy</u>   sympathy   pity   support   understanding)

13 COARSE   (refined   polite   fine   smooth   <u>rough</u>)

14 GYRATE   (strike   <u>slide</u>   swirl   count   pounce)

15 ESTEEM   (disrespect   <u>admire</u>   despise   mock   criticise)

Underline the pair of words most similar in meaning.

Example: come, go   <u>roam, wander</u>   fear, fare

16 wash, dry   bubble, soap   <u>twitter, babble</u>

17 <u>glimmer, glitter</u>   tinsel, tree   gloomy, cheerful

18 class, school   <u>type, category</u>   record, omission

19 <u>sumptuous, luxurious</u>   dull, sharp   wealthy, poor

20 consume, consider   breakfast, dinner   <u>peckish, hungry</u>

Test time: 0   5   10 minutes

Underline the two words which are the odd ones out in the following groups of words.

Example: black   king   purple   green   house

1	lane	path	pedestrian	car	way
2	gash	gush	rip	pour	slash
3	consider	think	considerable	large	substantial
4	trait	gift	feature	present	characteristic
5	graceful	lithe	awkward	elegant	bulky

Underline the one word in the brackets which will go equally well with both the pairs of words outside the brackets.

Example: rush, attack   cost, fee   (price, hasten, strike, <u>charge</u>, money)

6	confident, courageous	strong, striking	(paint, brave, bold, modest, vivid)
7	conceal, suppress	envelop, cloak	(replace, cover, insure, include, travel)
8	portrait, likeness	concept, idea	(picture, illustration, plan, painting, image)
9	recline, rest	untruth, fib	(falsehood, prostrate, lounge, lie, evade)
10	school, teach	locomotive, engine	(motor, steam, learn, train, develop)

Find a word that is similar to the word in capital letters and that rhymes with the second word.

Example: CABLE   tyre   ___wire___

11	ESCAPE	white	_____
12	FIRE	claim	flame
13	PURCHASED	caught	bought
14	ASCEND	rhyme	climb
15	DISBELIEVE	spout	doubt

Underline one word in the brackets which is most opposite in meaning to the word in capitals.

Example: WIDE   (broad   vague   long   <u>narrow</u>   motorway)

16	LIGHT	(flimsy	delicate	gentle	insubstantial	heavy)
17	REMARKABLE	(ordinary	astonishing	extraordinary	striking	exceptional)
18	HINDER	(delay	help	hamper	obstruct	instruct)
19	PAST	(gift	present	failed	ended	overtaken)
20	REMOTE	(distant	near	far	isolated	remove)

3

19/20   Total

Underline two words, one from each group, that go together to form a new word. The word in the first group always comes first.

Example: (hand, <u>green</u>, for)   (light, <u>house</u>, sure)

1 (<u>chop</u>, walk, dressing) (chair, path, <u>stick</u>)
3 (cereal, hole, <u>oat</u>) (bowl, meal, <u>wheat</u>)
2 (side, <u>out</u>, drop) (down, <u>law</u>, low)
4 (building, high, black) (<u>land</u>, gear, spot)

Find a word that can be put in front of each of the following words to make new, compound words.

Example: CAST   FALL   WARD   POUR   <u>DOWN</u>

5	BONE	WARD	DATE	FIRE	_____
6	BULB	LIGHT	BACK	CARD	_____
7	PIPE	SCREEN	WARD	SWEPT	_____
8	FLOWER	SHINE	TAN	BURN	_____

Find the letter which will complete both pairs of words, ending the first word and starting the second. The same letter must be used for both sets of words.

Example: mea (t) able   fi (t) ub

9 smu (_) rain   stin (___) rown   11 roo (_) ake   fil (_) eat
10 fla (_) est   cul (_) ent   12 stri (f) elt   shrim (_) ear

Complete the following expressions by underlining the missing word.

Example: Frog is to tadpole as swan is to (duckling, baby, <u>cygnet</u>).

13 Comfort is to distress as favour is to (support, prefer, <u>disapprove</u>).
14 Measure is to weigh as divide is to (<u>unite</u>, distribute, combine).
15 Ruler is to millimeter as clock is to (time, <u>minute</u>, hands).
16 Familiar is to usual as original is to (<u>novel</u>, ordinary, copied).

Underline the pair of words most opposite in meaning.

Example: cup, mug   coffee, milk   <u>hot, cold</u>

17	spin, revolve	circle, ring	<u>revolt, support</u>
18	erect, upright	build, construct	<u>assemble, dismantle</u>
19	<u>imperfect, flawless</u>	lacking, deficient	faulty, incomplete
20	benefit, handicap	advantage, asset	weakness, liability

4

Total 11/20

Test time: 0   5   10 minutes

Find the letter which will complete both pairs of words, ending the first word and starting the second. The same letter must be used for both sets of words.

Example: mea (t) able   fi (t) ub

1	bom	(b)	other		clim	(b)	reak
2	strang	(e)	ager		battl	(e)	mber
3	ironi	(c)	reak		mimi	(c)	aste
4	cal	(~~s~~)	leet		snif	(___)	rank

Find two letters which will end the first word and start the second word.

Example: rea (c h) air

5	tr	(e e)	rie		7	bea	(___ ___)	ips
6	ba	(c k)	ink		8	trif	(l e)	ather

Add one letter to the word in capital letters to make a new word. The meaning of the new word is given in the clue.

Example: PLAN   simple   ___PLAIN___

9	RAFT	skill	_craft_	11	SOON	utensil	_spoon_
10	WEED	cloth	_____	12	TIED	weary	_tired_

Move one letter from the first word and add it to the second word to make two new words.

Example: hunt   sip   ___hut___   ___snip___

13	patient	bran	_____	_____
14	wring	swam	_____	_____
15	parking	night	_____	_____
16	breathe	spin	_____	_____

Change the first word into the last word, by changing one letter at a time and making two new, different words in the middle.

Example: TEAK   ___TEAT___   ___TENT___   RENT

17	CROW	_____	_____	LOOP
18	KNOB	_____	_____	UNIT
19	SPIN	_____	_____	SLUR
20	MAZE	_____	_____	NICE

Total ___

Test time: 0   5   10 minutes

Rearrange the letters in capitals to make another word. The new word has something to do with the first two words.

Example: spot, soil   SAINT   __STAIN__

1   scanty, scarce   SPARES   _____

2   eats, feasts   SNIDE   _Dines_____

3   misery, dejection   PRAISED   _____

4   chief, main   PASTEL   _____

5   issue, provide   PIQUE   _____

6   lift, hoist   REVEL   _____

Find and underline the two words which need to change places for the sentence to make sense.

Example: She went to <u>letter</u> the <u>write</u>.

7   One <u>can</u> swim over she thousand metres.

8   Mixing green and yellow paint makes blue.

9   The room entered the <u>children</u> quietly and sat on the floor.

10   The <u>sitting</u> in the <u>carpet</u> room is too patterned.

11   It was raining <u>outside hard.</u>

12   Perhaps <u>you</u> can stay with I?

Look at the first group of three words. The word in the middle has been made from the other two words. Complete the second group of three words in the same way, making a new word in the middle.

Example: PAIN   INTO   TOOK   ALSO   __SOON__   ONLY

13	HIKE	KEEP	EPIC	MOST	stun	UNTO
14	BIRO	BIND	POND	TRAY	TRIP	FLIP
15	WORE	WINE	PINT	PORT	part	CARS
16	READ	YEAR	YARD	GLUE	BENE	BEEN
17	KIND	KILL	PULL	BOOK	Booh	WITH
18	MAZE	SAME	MISS	TINY	MISY	CAMP
19	TAKE	FLAT	FOOL	YARD	BRAY	BOAR
20	BUSH	WISH	WICK	PILE	F	PONY

6

Total 13/20

Test time: 0 | | | | | 5 | | | | | 10 minutes

Find the four-letter word hidden at the end of one word and the beginning of the next word. The order of the letters may not be changed.

Example: The children had bats and balls. _____sand_____

✗1 Please remember to close the yellow door. _____seth_____

C2 That old man is my grandfather. _____told_____

F3 Fragments of dinosaur bone are scattered there. _____~~weat~~._____

(4 My teacher corrects our work every day. _____s our_____

✗5 The photographer's work is hung in this room. _____swor_____

C6 You should lift the books carefully. _____scare_____

✗7 Seamus did not enjoy the party. _____epav_____

C8 That bus arrives too soon for John to catch. _____

Find the three-letter word which can be added to the letters in capitals to make a new word. The new word will complete the sentence sensibly.

✗Example: The cat sprang onto the MO. _____USE_____

9 The skater was able to GE along the ice with grace. _____T_____

10 He ate up his carrots and CABE. _____gge_____

11 Kittens are extremely PFUL. _____

12 As the sun comes from behind the clouds, the sky LIGHS. _____

13 The ENTCE to the palace was very grand. _____

14 A THERMOER is an instrument for measuring temperature. _____

Find the four-letter word which can be added to the letters in capitals to make a new word. The new word will complete the sentence sensibly.

Example: At the zoo, we visited the REP house. _____TILE_____

15 The students liked the teacher because he was very CING. _____

16 The ducklings were FOLLO their mother across the pond. _____Wing_____

17 Someone who does not tell lies is HO. _____nest_____

18 The chef GD the carrot into slivers for the salad. _____t_____

19 "Would Troy please RE to the school office." _____turn_____

20 At the class reunion people felt SENNTAL when the songs from their school days were played. _____

7

Total [5/20]

A B C D E F G H I J K L M N O P Q R S T U V W X Y Z

Fill in the missing letters. The alphabet has been written out to help you.

Example: AB is to CD as PQ is to _RS_

1   TV is to QS as FH is to   ____

2   QY is to RZ as SA is to   ____

3   GH is to FI as ST is to   ____

4   GD is to EB as CZ is to   ____

5   DW is to EV as HS is to   ____

A B C D E F G H I J K L M N O P Q R S T U V W X Y Z

Give the missing letters and numbers in the following sequences. The alphabet has been written out to help you.

Example: CQ   DQ   EP   FP   _GO_   _HO_

6	RG	RF	RE	SD	SC	____
7	aV	dT	____	jP	____	pL
8	X3	Y4	Z5	A6	B7	C8
9	17T	15T	13S	11S	9Π	7R
10	XD	____	ZF	____	BH	CI

Give the two missing numbers in the following sequences.

Example: 2   4   6   _8_   _10_

11	2	3	5	8	12	17
12	2	4	8	16	32	64
13	29	16	17	18	17	16
14	16	21	26	31	36	41
15	17	18	19	16	17	18

If a = 8, b = 6, c = 4, d = 3 and e = 2, find the value of the following calculations. Write your answer as a letter.

16   $\dfrac{ab}{c}$ – de   12 – 3   =   _6_

17   bd ÷ b   18 – 12   =   _3_

18   (a + b + c) – cd   =   _6_

19   b^2 – ac   36 – 32   =   _4_

20   $\dfrac{b^2}{d^2}$ × e $\dfrac{36}{9}$ 4+   =   _8_

(8)

A B C D E F G H I J K L M N O P Q R S T U V W X Y Z

Fill in the missing letters. The alphabet has been written out to help you.

Example: AB is to CD as PQ is to <u>RS</u>

1 UX is to VY as WZ is to ____

2 AZ is to CX as HS is to ____

3 HJ is to LN as RT is to ____

4 QM is to TP as UQ is to ____

5 HL is to GH as NR is to ____

A B C D E F G H I J K L M N O P Q R S T U V W X Y Z

Give the missing letters and numbers in the following sequences. The alphabet has been written out to help you.

Example: CQ DQ EP FP <u>GO</u> <u>HO</u>

6	____	Z10	A15	B20	____	D30
7	PN	QO	____	____	TR	US
8	10I	____	12K	____	14M	15M
9	____	BY	CX	____	EV	FU
10	aJb	____	eNf	gPh	____	kTl

Give the two missing numbers in the following sequences.

Example: 2 4 6 <u>8</u> <u>10</u>

11	58	57	55	____	____	43
12	2	5	8	____	14	____
13	53	____	____	32	25	18
14	5	____	9	8	____	12
15	3	6	____	24	48	____

If p = 7, q = 3, r = 20, s = 5 and t = 15, find the value of the following calculations.

16 $2p - (q + s)$ = ____

17 $(r + s) \times (p - q)$ = ____

18 $s^2 + r + 2t$ = ____

19 $\dfrac{pr - (r + t)}{s}$ = ____

20 $\dfrac{qr}{s} + t$ = ____

9

Here are the codes for four words. Work out which code matches each word.

7 ^ 3 *	6 * ^ 3	7 * ^ 6	7 ^ 3 6
NEAR	BEAN	BARN	BARE

1   7 ^ 3 *   _____   **3**   7 * ^ 6   _____

2   6 * ^ 3   _____   **4**   7 ^ 3 6   _____

Using the same code, encode these words:

5   EARN   _____   **6**   ARENA   _____

Work out the following codes.

7   If the code for SQUARE is USWCTG, what is the code for DICED?   _____

8   If the code for POLICE is QPMJDF, what is the code for SPEED?   _____

9   If the code for LETTER is JCRRCP, what is the code for NOTES?   _____

10   If the code for WONDER is VNMCDQ, what is the code for SWISH?   _____

Pete has planted his vegetable garden in rows by his father's greenhouse. Using the information below, work out which vegetable is grown in each row.

A
B
C
CARROTS
E
F
G

GREENHOUSE

The lettuces and radishes are next to each other but neither is next to the carrots or the onions. The peas are next to the carrots. The herbs are closest to the greenhouse. The spinach is between the radishes and the carrots.

11–16   A = _____   D = CARROTS   G = _____

B = _____   E = _____

C = _____   F = _____

If November has five Sundays and the last Sunday is on the final day of the month, calculate the following:

17   What is the date of the first Sunday of the month?   _____

18   What day of the week is 3rd November?   _____

19   What date is the fourth Wednesday?   _____

20   Which other day of the week, beside Sunday, has five days in this November?   _____

(10)

Total

If G = 2, R = 6, O = 7, E = 4, T = 5 and S = 3, find the sum of the following words by adding their letters together.

1	OGRE _____	**3**	ROOT _____	**5**	STORE _____
2	SORE _____	**4**	TREES _____		

A B C D E F G H I J K L M N O P Q R S T U V W X Y Z

Fill in the missing letters. The alphabet has been written out to help you.

Example: AB is to CD as PQ is to RS

6	KN is to OR as VY is to ____	**9**	TW is to XY as GJ is to ____
7	JM is to PS as BE is to ____	**10**	DW is to GT as JQ is to ____
8	WU is to SQ as JH is to ____	**11**	DH is to CD as TX is to ____

Read the first two statements and then underline one of the four options below that must be true.

12 'Tony loves chocolate bars. Chocco bars are his favourite.'
- A   Chocco bars are the only type of chocolate bars that Tony buys.
- B   Chocco bars are a type of chocolate bar.
- C   Tony's favourites snacks are chocolate bars.
- D   Tony eats chocolate bars most days.

13 'My father catches the train to London every day. Often the train is late.'
- A   My father's train is often late.
- B   My father is often late for the train.
- C   The train to London is late every day.
- D   The train from London is often late.

If e=9, f=2, g=10, h=5 and i=0, find the value of the following calculations:

14 $(e + f) \times i =$ _____

15 $\dfrac{g}{h} \times f =$ _____

16 $g^2 + f^2 =$ _____

17 $(h + i) \times (e - f) =$ _____

The next Tuesday after:

18 Wednesday 16th September is _____.

19 Tuesday 27th October is _____.

20 Sunday 29th November is _____.

Total

Test time: 0   5   10 minutes

Underline two words, one from each group, that go together to form a new word. The word in the first group always comes first.

Example: (hand, <u>green</u>, for)   (light, <u>house</u>, sure)

1   (where, when, which)   (as, if, over)
2   (climb, stood, dug)   (off, in, out)
3   (by, con, in)   (war, test, low)
4   (low, par, give)   (take, way, many)

Rearrange the letters in capitals to make another word. The new word has something to do with the first two words.

Example: spot, soil   SAINT   _STAIN_

5   javelin, lance   REAPS   _____
6   stationed, displayed   DESPOT   _____
7   response, reply   CREATION   _____
8   diagram, plan   SINGED   _____
9   broom, sweeper   SHRUB   _____

Underline the word in the brackets which goes best with the words given outside the brackets.

Example: word, paragraph, sentence   (pen, cap, <u>letter</u>, top, stop)

10   suddenly, unexpectedly, abruptly   (soon, loudly, quickly, clearly, mistakenly)
11   deduct, remove, diminish   (divide, decimal, add, subtract, percentage)
12   penalty, forfeit, fine   (goal, game, punishment, reward, rule)
13   fur, fleece, coat   (comb, head, hairstyle, stroke, pelt)
14   chase, hunt, trail   (look, chide, wound, pursue, climb)

Here are some codes for four words. Work out which code matches which word.

# / < ~	# / ~ ~	< / ~ >	~ < / >
PAST	MAPS	MASS	SPAT

15   PAST   _____   17   MASS   _____
16   MAPS   _____   18   SPAT   _____

Encode: Decode:

19   STAMP   _____   20   ~ < / ~ #   _____

12

Underline the two words which are the odd ones out in the following groups of words.

Example: black   <u>king</u>   purple   green   <u>house</u>

1	train	track	coach	instruct	rail
2	head	foot	chief	principal	mind
3	crucial	vital	unnecessary	key	lock
4	raspberry	strawberry	peach	cherry	blackberry
5	ask	beg	beseech	implore	query

Find the three-letter word which can be added to the letters in capitals to make a new word. The new word will complete the sentence sensibly.

Example: The cat sprang onto the MO. ___USE___

6   The pirate had a CH over one eye.   _____

7   "There is too much CTER in this classroom" said the teacher.   _____

8   Red Riding Hood's grandmother lived in a COTT deep in
the woods.   _____

9   When you FR, your brow wrinkles.   _____

10   A rat is a type of ROT.   _____

Remove one letter from the word in capital letters to leave a new word. The meaning of the new word is given in the clue.

Example: AUNT   an insect   ___ANT___

11   PLIGHT   illuminate   _____

12   TWINGE   string   _____

13   LEATHER   soap   _____

14   HOISTED   entertained   _____

Give the two missing numbers in the following sequences.

Example: 2   4   6   <u>8</u>   <u>10</u>

15	19	18	16	___	9	___
16	13	___	19	22	___	28
17	6	7	9	___	___	3
18	___	42	___	28	21	14
19	___	___	20	22	25	27
20	128	___	32	___	8	4

13

Total

TEST 13: **Mixed**

Craig's birthday is on 4th February. Toby's birthday is one week before Craig's and three weeks before Frank's.

1 When is Toby's birthday? _____

2 When is Frank's birthday? _____

3 If I break up from school on Tuesday 29th July and I go back to school on Wednesday 3rd September, how many weeks' holiday do I have? _____

4 How many days altogether in September and October? _____

Benjamin went to the dentist on a Tuesday. He has two further appointments for fillings. One is ten days later, the next is five days after the second appointment. On which days of the week are the following appointments?

5 the second appointment _____

6 the third appointment _____

Find a word that is similar in meaning to the word in capital letters and that rhymes with the second word.

Example: CABLE   tyre   ___wire___

7   DISH   roll   _____

8   BENEATH   wonder   _____

9   HORSE   hair   _____

10 AFFLUENT   ditch   _____

11 AIM   joint   _____

Rearrange the muddled letters in capitals to make a proper word. The answer will complete the sentence sensibly.

Example: A BEZAR is an animal with stripes.   ___ZEBRA___

12 A CHITNEK is a room in a house.   _____

13 Would you like a TTSEOAD cheese sandwich?   _____

14 Her birthday is on the GTHIEH.   _____

15 A GTFHI broke out between the boys.   _____

16 This morning it is bright and SFRYOT. _____

Find the letter which will end the first word and start the second word.

Example: peac (h) ome

17 stran (____) ebt   **19** stra (____) hinny

18 fad   (____) ats   **20** thum (____) athe

Total _____

Underline the one word in the brackets which will go equally well with both the pairs of words outside the brackets.

Example: rush, attack   cost, fee   (price, hasten, strike, <u>charge</u>, money)

1   lessen, reduce   brighten, illuminate   (decrease, shade, lighten, lose, subtract)

2   opening, break   pierce, puncture   (fissure, hole, perforate, whole, deflate)

3   lord, noble   gape, gaze   (duke, vision, stare, look, peer)

4   coerce, compel   build, construct   (impel, produce, cause, gain, make)

5   head, features   confront, tackle   (handle, object, face, note, manage)

Complete the following sentences by selecting the most sensible word from each group of words given in the brackets. Underline the word selected.

Example: The (<u>children</u>, books, foxes) carried the (houses, <u>books</u>, steps) home from the (greengrocer, <u>library</u>, factory).

6   My baby (caterpillar, bird, brother) crawls down the (lift, stairs, bus) (tomorrow, backwards, table).

7   It has rained so (slowly, little, heavily) the (bus, hill, river) has (flooded, swum, drowned).

8   Please (close, break, open) the (parcel, window, rule), Gavin, as it is (Sunday, cold, noon).

9   When the postman (knocks, eats, smiles) our (cat, clock, dog) (barks, neighs, chimes).

A B C D E F G H I J K L M N O P Q R S T U V W X Y Z

Fill in the missing letters. The alphabet has been written out to help you.

Example: AB is to CD as PQ is to RS

10   LI is to KH as DA is to ____   **13**   GJ is to FK as QT is to ____

11   MP is to MJ as FI is to ____   **14**   MN is to KP as JQ is to ____

12   QP is to ML as JI is to ____   **15**   LH is to OK as PL is to ____

If u = 16, v = 12, w = 10, j = 5, y = 4 and z = 2, find the value of the following calculations. Write your answer as a letter.

16 $(j^2 - u) - y$ =   _____

17 $\dfrac{yw}{j} + z$ =   _____

18 $\dfrac{u + v + y}{z}$ =   _____

19 $\dfrac{(vz + y^2)}{j} + z$ =   _____

20 $(6j - 2v) + y$ =   _____

15

Total

Test 15: Mixed

Test time: 0 ... 5 ... 10 minutes

Find a word that can be put in front of each of the following words to make new, compound words.

Example: CAST   FALL   WARD   POUR   ___DOWN___

1	BROW	LIGHT	LAND	LIGHTER	_____
2	POWER	GROVE	AGE	HOLE	_____
3	BOW	FIRE	ROADS	BAR	_____
4	MARE	GOWN	CLUB	LIFE	_____

Find and underline the two words which need to change places for the sentence to make sense.

Example: She went to <u>letter</u> the <u>write</u>.

5   He climbed the stairs slowly as he did not go to want to bed.

6   Michelle fell over in her playground and cut the knee badly.

7   Britain's changeable is climate.

8   Blisters can occur when your feet or shoes rub your boots.

9   Tina's mother gives her break to eat at fruit.

The fish counter in my local supermarket is laid out like this:

LEFT   RIGHT

A	B	C	D	E	F

From the information below, work out which type of fish goes into each tray.

The salmon steaks are between the cod and tuna steaks. The sea bream is directly to the left of the cod but to the right of the halibut. The plaice is next to the tuna steaks on the right.

10	salmon	____	**13**	sea bream	____
11	cod	____	**14**	halibut	____
12	tuna	____	**15**	plaice	____

If the code for CONSTANTLY is * ! $ £ ^ @ $ ^ > %, decode these words:

16   £ ^ ! $ %   _____   **18** $ @ £ ^ %   _____

17   * > @ £ £   _____

Using the same code, encode these words:

19   STOOL   _____   **20**   COTTON   _____

16
Total

Test 16: Mixed

Underline two words, one from each group, that go together to form a new word. The word in the first group always comes first.

Example: (hand, <u>green</u>, for)   (light, <u>house</u>, sure)

1   (take, name, part)   (more, less, some)
2   (west, hospital, double)   (bed, size, ward)
3   (high, counter, leaf)   (wheel, game, act)
4   (tar, tear, give)   (man, son, get)

A B C D E F G H I J K L M N O P Q R S T U V W X Y Z

5   If the code for SERMON is UGTOQP, what is the code for TALKS?   _____
6   If the code for SUBTLE is RTASKD, what is the code for QUICK?   _____
7   If the code for PARCEL is SZUBHK, what is the code for GIFTS?   _____
8   If the code for ANGELS is ZOFFKT, what is the code for STARS?   _____
9   If the code for CHAIRS is YDWENO, what is the code for TABLE?   _____

Underline one word in the brackets which is most opposite in meaning to the word in capitals.

Example: WIDE   (broad   vague   long   <u>narrow</u>   motorway)

10   REMEMBER   (recall   recollect   forget   forgive   foretell)
11   CHARM   (repel   captivate   dazzle   enchant   delight)
12   CONFIDENT   (bold   courageous   timid   valiant   vacant)
13   ROUGH   (bumpy   gentle   rowdy   smother   brutal)
14   APPEAR   (emerge   materialise   hide   disappoint   vanish)

Find a word that is similar in meaning to the word in capital letters and that rhymes with the second word.

15   BOTHER   rubble   _____   17   GENTLE   wild _____
16   COUNTERFEIT   make   _____

Three friends are all taking their driving test in the same month, April. Zita takes it first, nine days before Tony. Zoe takes her test on the second-last day of the month and exactly two weeks after Tony.

18   Zita takes her test on _____.   20   Zoe takes her test on _____.
19   Tony takes his test on _____.

Total _____

Rearrange the muddled letters in capitals to make a proper word. The answer will complete the sentence sensibly.

Example: A BEZAR is an animal with stripes.   <u>ZEBRA</u>

1   Their school MOUFNIR is green.   _____

2   CRUMEYR is the planet closest to the sun.   _____

3   You look as if you have been dragged through a DEGHE backwards.   _____

4   The city centre was congested with FACTFIR.   _____

5   Three times five is TEFFINE.   _____

Underline the word in the brackets which goes best with the words given outside the brackets.

Example: word, paragraph, sentence   (pen, cap, <u>letter</u>, top, stop)

6   worry, anxiety   (relaxed, calmness, peaceful, relieved, apprehension)

7   scenic, picturesque   (country, view, sketch, play, attractive)

8   peep, peek   (stare, study, temper, glance, gape)

9   bleak, bare   (cold, plentiful, stark, clue, abundant)

10   actual, genuine   (authentic, fake, false, dishonest, bogus)

Remove one letter from the word in capital letters to leave a new word. The meaning of the new word is given in the clue.

Example: AUNT   an insect   <u>ANT</u>

11   QUITE   leave   _____

12   BRANCH   large farm   _____

13   WITCH   tickle   _____

14   CLAIM   mollusc   _____

Give the two missing numbers in the following sequences.

Example: 2   4   6   <u>8</u>   <u>10</u>

15	2	3	___	4	6	___	
16	___	___	20	40	80	160	
17	3	7	11	___	___	23	
18	1	3	6	8	___	___	
19	3	___	8	4	___	6	
20	17	16	___	11	7	___	

Total _____

A B C D E F G H I J K L M N O P Q R S T U V W X Y Z

1 If the code for BOTHER is ANSGDQ, what is the code for TRUTH? _____

2 If the code for PRAYER is QSBZFS, what is the code for CHANT? _____

3 If the code for SAILED is UCKNGF, what is the code for YACHT? _____

4 If the code for PENCIL is NCLAGJ, what is the code for RULER? _____

5 If the code for CLUTCH is AMSUAI, what is the code for BRAKE? _____

6 If the code for BOTTLE is ZMRRJC, what is the code for WATER? _____

Underline the two words which are the odd ones out in the following groups of words.

Example: black   <u>king</u>   purple   green   <u>house</u>

7	imposing	magnificent	impostor	splendid	magnify
8	eye	ear	knee	hip	elbow
9	tear	cry	howl	wail	noise
10	beat	pound	pence	pancake	batter
11	wash	bathe	basket	bowl	write

Fill in the crosswords so that all the given words are included. You have been given one letter as a clue in each crossword.

12–15

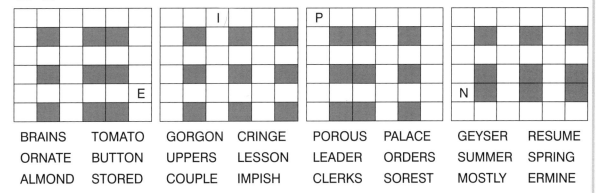

BRAINS	TOMATO	GORGON	CRINGE	POROUS	PALACE	GEYSER	RESUME
ORNATE	BUTTON	UPPERS	LESSON	LEADER	ORDERS	SUMMER	SPRING
ALMOND	STORED	COUPLE	IMPISH	CLERKS	SOREST	MOSTLY	ERMINE

Find the letter which will end the first word and start the second word.

Example: peac (h) ome

16 plan (___) go   **19** whar (___) ate

17 slan (___) hrow   **20** medi (___) rime

18 benc (___) orde

Total [_____]

Underline the one word in the brackets which will go equally well with both the pairs of words outside the brackets.

Example: rush, attack   cost, fee   (price, hasten, strike, <u>charge</u>, money)

1	blaze, inferno	shoot, discharge	(flames, fire, launch, gun, burning)
2	delicate, faint	underweight, flimsy	(gentle, soft, light, pale, fade)
3	fleck, spot	celebrate, observe	(speck, stamp, dot, seal, mark)
4	skin, pelt	camouflage, cloak	(hide, lose, conceal, cover, jacket)
5	name, label	shout, cry	(identify, yell, screech, call, brand)

Complete the following sentences in the best way by choosing one word from each set of brackets.

Example: Tall is to (tree, <u>short</u>, colour) as narrow is to (thin, white, <u>wide</u>).

6   Play is to (scene, audience, ticket) as book is to (chapter, cover, author).

7   Wolf is to (dog, pack, wild) as goose is to (feather, beak, flock).

8   Cow is to (milk, farm, bull) as duck is to (feather, drake, fly).

9   Minor is to (age, lesser, main) as favourite is to (preferred, inferior, secondary).

In a code, if A = 1, B = 2, C = 3 and so on, encode these words:

10   HEDGE   _____   **12**   CABBAGE   _____

11   FACED   _____

Using the same code, decode these:

13   31754   _____   **15**   21475   _____

14   61454   _____

Find and underline the two words which need to change places for the sentence to make sense.

Example: She went to <u>letter</u> the <u>write</u>.

16   At the weekend we often have gravy meat, vegetables and roast.

17   My father ate her lunch with my aunt in the garden.

18   As the storm raged, the rocks crashed against the waves.

19   Twickenham is the rugby of English home.

20   My grandmother's chime has a very loud clock.

Total

TEST 20: Mixed

Test time: 0   5   10 minutes

Find a word that can be put in front of each of the following words to make new, compound words.

Example: CAST   FALL   WARD   POUR   ___DOWN___

1	SOME	SHAKE	CUFF	WRITING	_____
2	BURST	SIDE	LINE	BREAK	_____
3	SHED	WIND	WORK	PECKER	_____
4	BOAT	STYLE	TIME	LINE	_____

Change the first word of the third pair in the same way as the other pairs to give a new word.

Example: bind, hind   bare, hare   but, ___hut___

5	dark, bark	drain, brain	drake, _____
6	cram, arm	hilt, lit	test, _____
7	castanets, cats	cartridge, cage	carbonise, _____
8	society, cosy	crash, arch	mature, _____
9	stencil, nets	stellar, lets	stepfather, _____

If the code for VEGETABLE is 938316253, decode the following words:

10   265531   _____

11   96593   _____

Using the same code, encode these words:

12   BLEAT   _____

13   GABLE   _____

14   LEAVE   _____

Work out the following codes.

15   If the code for SWITCH is TXJUDI, what does DMBNQ stand for?   _____

16   If the code for BEETLE is ADDSKD, what does VNQLR stand for?   _____

17   If the code for TREATS is VTGCVU, what does VWTPU stand for?   _____

18   If the code for WASHES is UYQFCQ, what is the code for BASIN?   _____

19   If the code for DREAMS is FQGZOR, what is the code for SIZES?   _____

20   If the code for BEATEN is ZFYUCO, what is the code for SORRY?   _____

Total

Underline the pair of words most opposite in meaning.

Example: cup, mug   coffee, milk   <u>hot, cold</u>

1	neglect, nurture	strike, knock	ignore, overlook
2	doubtful, distrustful	trusting, wary	dubious, suspect
3	basin, bath	float, sink	hot, warm
4	many, few	numerous, plentiful	best, finest

Look at the first group of three words. The word in the middle has been made from the other two words. Complete the second group of three words in the same way, making a new word in the middle.

Example: PAIN   INTO   TOOK   ALSO   <u>SOON</u>   ONLY

5	WANT	SENT	SEAL	MOTH	_____	PALE
6	PACE	PART	TRIM	FLIP	_____	WEST
7	SOON	SIGN	HIGH	FEET	_____	LACE
8	KILN	KIND	NEED	SUCH	_____	ROPE
9	HINT	THIN	HAND	HARP	_____	RAYS

Underline the word in the brackets which goes best with the words given outside the brackets.

Example: word, paragraph, sentence   (pen, cap, <u>letter</u>, top, stop)

10	gentle, mild	(rough, placid, extreme, forceful, violent)
11	muddle, tangle	(organised, jumble, structured, tidy, neat)
12	house, bungalow	(castle, palace, mansion, hotel, cottage)
13	sodden, drenched	(burnt, scorched, soaked, damp, dry)
14	previous, former	(later, subsequent, next, prior, last)

A B C D E F G H I J K L M N O P Q R S T U V W X Y Z

Give the missing letters and numbers in the following sequences.
The alphabet has been written out to help you.

Example: CQ   DQ   EP   FP   <u>GO</u>   <u>HO</u>

15	____	Rs8	Pu7	____	Ly5	Ja4
16	JCA	KCC	____	KDG	____	KDK
17	MN	____	KP	____	IR	HS
18	bde	fhi	____	npq	____	vxy
19	25A	____	17Y	13X	9W	____
20	____	TZ	WY	ZX	____	FV

Total [   ]

TEST 22: Mixed

Find and underline the two words which need to change places for the sentence to make sense.

Example: She went to <u>letter</u> the <u>write</u>.

1   On Friday night, Peter to going is the cinema.

2   My father straightens the tie in front of his hall mirror.

3   The traffic led as the duck stopped her ducklings across the road.

4   In school, we play football after the park.

5   In the distance, I could see a hot sky balloon high in the air.

Underline the two words which are the odd ones out in the following groups of words.

Example: black   <u>king</u>   purple   green   <u>house</u>

6	petrol	cap	bonnet	wheel	beret
7	find	weigh	track	follow	trail
8	below	beneath	between	beyond	under
9	pass	grade	fail	rank	rate
10	sporadic	often	infrequent	periodic	regular

Move one letter from the first word and add it to the second word to make two new words.

Example: hunt   sip   _____hut_____   _____snip_____

11   grasping   fail   _____   _____

12   rare   pawns   _____   _____

13   splint   wader   _____   _____

14   finger   thin   _____   _____

Give the two missing numbers in the following sequences.

Example: 2   4   6   _8_   _10_

15	2	11	4	___	6	5	___	2
16	13	___	16	17	19	___	22	23
17	___	2	___	7	11	16		
18	8	11	___	17	___	23		
19	96	48	24	___	6	___		
20	15	___	11	7	___	4	3	1

(23)

Total

Test time: 0   5   10 minutes

My grandmother's sewing box has nine compartments. The cottons are in the top right and the middle left compartments. The pins are in the bottom middle one. Work out where the other items go:

TOP

1	2	3 Cottons
4 Cottons	5	6
7	8 Pins	9

BOTTOM

My grandmother kept the needles next to the pins and the thimble next to the needles. The tape measure is not next to the pins. The folding scissors are above one of the cotton compartments. The buttons are not next to the needles. The pincushion is kept next to the pins and one of the cottons.

1	needles	____	**3**	tape measure	____	**5**	buttons	____
2	thimble	____	**4**	scissors	____	**6**	pincushion	____

Underline the word in the brackets which is most opposite in meaning to the word in capitals.

Example: WIDE   (broad   vague   long   <u>narrow</u>   motorway)

7	APPRECIATE	(neglect	prize	esteem	respect	value)
8	TIDY	(neat	messy	seaside	orderly	untied)
9	TIRED	(wheel	exhausted	sleepy	stale	rested)
10	AMIABLE	(friendly	unfriendly	kind	agreeable	affable)
11	WONDERFUL	(fabulous	fantastic	dreadful	amazing	joyous)

A B C D E F G H I J K L M N O P Q R S T U V W X Y Z

12   If the code for BATTER is ^ @ / / = £, decode ^ = / / = £.   _____

13   If the code for TREBLE is 748918, decode 98487.   _____

14   If the code for WINTER is XJPQFN, decode NFPFX.   _____

15   If the code for CRADLE is ~ @ / # ? !, decode ? / @ # ! @.   _____

16   If the code for FASTER is ! I 7 4 $ X, decode 7 I ! $ X.   _____

Find the letter which will complete both pairs of words, ending the first word and starting the second. The same letter must be used for both sets of words.

Example: mea (t) able   fi (t) ub

17	tin	(___)	awn	part	(___)	ellow
18	tea	(___)	ight	cella	(___)	ode
19	war	(___)	ought	bee	(___)	oun
20	bras	(___)	ire	peris	(___)	ound

Total

Answers

TEST 1: SORTING WORDS 1

1 gossip	12 jealousy
2 invent	13 rough
3 precise	14 swirl
4 disgrace	15 admire
5 protect	16 twitter, babble
6 eager, enthusiastic	17 glimmer, glitter
7 crisis, dilemma	18 type, category
8 charge, entrust	19 sumptuous, luxurious
9 perish, die	20 peckish, hungry
10 enrage, infuriate	
11 mouldy	

TEST 2: SORTING WORDS 2

1 pedestrian, car	10 train
2 gush, pour	11 flight
3 consider, think	12 flame
4 gift, present	13 bought
5 awkward, bulky	14 climb
6 bold	15 doubt
7 cover	16 heavy
8 image	17 ordinary
9 lie	18 help
	19 present
	20 near

TEST 3: SELECTING WORDS 1

1 chopstick	14 distribute
2 outlaw	15 minute
3 oatmeal	16 novel
4 highland	17 revolt, support
5 BACK	18 assemble, dismantle
6 FLASH	19 imperfect, flawless
7 WIND	20 benefit, handicap
8 SUN	
9 g 11 m	
10 t 12 p	
13 disapprove	

TEST 4: SELECTING WORDS 2

1 b	3 c	5 ee	7 ch
2 e	4 f	6 th	8 le

9 CRAFT	16 breath, spine
10 TWEED	
11 SPOON	17 CROP, COOP
12 TIRED	
13 patent, brain	18 KNOT, KNIT
14 wing, swarm	19 SPUN, SPUR
15 paring, knight	20 MACE, MICE

TEST 5: ANAGRAMS 1

1 SPARSE	11 outside, hard
2 DINES	
3 DESPAIR	12 you, I
4 STAPLE	13 STUN
5 EQUIP	14 TRIP
6 LEVER	15 PART
7 One, she	16 BLUE
8 green, blue	17 BOTH
9 room, children	18 PITY
	19 BRAY
10 sitting, carpet	20 POLE

TEST 6: ANAGRAMS 2

1 they	8 vest	15 HARM
2 told	9 LID	16 WING
3 near	10 BAG	17 NEST
4 sour	11 LAY	18 RATE
5 shun	12 TEN	19 PORT
6 scar	13 RAN	20 TIME
7 note	14 MET	

TEST 7: CODED SEQUENCES AND LOGIC 1

1 CE	7 gR, mN	14 16, 26
2 TB	8 A6, C8	15 14, 21
3 RU	9 17T, 13S	16 b
4 AX	10 YE, AG	17 d
5 IR	11 5, 17	18 b
6 RF, SB	12 4, 16	19 c
	13 23, 20	20 a

TEST 8: CODED SEQUENCES AND LOGIC 2

1 XA	6 Y5, C25	11 52, 48
2 JQ	7 RP, SQ	12 11, 17
3 VX	8 11I, 13K	13 46, 39
4 XT	9 AZ, DW	14 4, 13
5 MN	10 cLd, iRj	15 12, 96

16 6	18 75	20 27	
17 100	19 21		

TEST 9: CODED SEQUENCES AND LOGIC 3

1 BARE	12 B = radishes
2 NEAR	
3 BEAN	13 C = spinach
4 BARN	14 E = peas
5 * ^ 3 6	15 F = onions
6 ^ 3 * 6 ^	16 G = herbs
7 FKEGF	17 2nd
8 TQFFE	18 Monday
9 LMRCQ	19 26th
10 RVHRG	20 Saturday
11 A = lettuces	

TEST 10: CODED SEQUENCES AND LOGIC 4

1 19	7 HK	13 A
2 20	8 FD	14 0
3 25	9 KL	15 4
4 22	10 MN	16 104
5 25	11 ST	17 35
6 ZC	12 B	
18 22nd September		
19 3rd November		
20 1st December		

TEST 11: MIXED

1 whereas	11 subtract
2 dugout	12 punishment
3 contest	13 pelt
4 partake	14 pursue
5 SPEAR	15 < / ~ >
6 POSTED	16 # / < ~
7 REACTION	17 # / ~ ~
8 DESIGN	18 ~ < / >
9 BRUSH	19 ~ > / # <
10 quickly	20 SPASM

TEST 12: MIXED

1 track, rail	7 HAT
2 foot, mind	8 AGE
3 unnecessary, lock	9 OWN
	10 DEN
4 peach, cherry	11 LIGHT
5 ask, query	12 TWINE
6 PAT	13 LATHER
	14 HOSTED

14 HOSTED   18 49, 35
15 13, 4   19 15, 17
16 16, 25   20 64, 16
17 5, 12

TEST 13: MIXED

1 28th January	10 rich
2 18th February	11 point
3 5	12 KITCHEN
4 61	13 TOASTED
5 Friday	14 EIGHTH
6 Wednesday	15 FIGHT
7 bowl	16 FROSTY
8 under	17 d 19 w
9 mare	18 e 20 b

TEST 14: MIXED

1 lighten	9 knocks, dog, barks
2 hole	
3 peer	10 CZ
4 make	11 FC
5 face	12 FE
6 brother, stairs, backwards	13 PU
	14 HS
7 heavily, river, flooded	15 SO
	16 j 19 w
8 close, window, cold	17 w 20 w
	18 u

TEST 15: MIXED

1 HIGH	11 C
2 MAN	12 E
3 CROSS	13 B
4 NIGHT	14 A
5 go, want	15 F
6 her, the	16 STONY
7 changeable, climate	17 CLASS
8 feet, boots	18 NASTY
9 break, fruit	19 £ ^ ! ! >
10 D	20 * ! ^ ^ ! $

TEST 16: MIXED

1 nameless	7 JHISV
2 westward	8 RUZSR
3 counteract	9 PWXHA
4 target	10 forget
5 VCNMU	11 repel
6 PTHBJ	12 timid

13 gentle   17 mild
14 vanish   18 6th April
15 trouble   19 15th April
16 fake   20 29th April

TEST 17: MIXED

1 UNIFORM	11 QUIT
2 MERCURY	12 RANCH
3 HEDGE	13 ITCH
4 TRAFFIC	14 CLAM
5 FIFTEEN	15 4, 5
6 apprehension	16 5, 10
7 attractive	17 15, 19
8 glance	18 11, 13
9 stark	19 2, 13
10 authentic	20 14, 2

TEST 18: MIXED

1 SQTSG
2 DIBOU
3 ACEJV
4 PSJCP
5 ZSYLC
6 UYRCP
7 impostor, magnify
8 eye, ear
9 tear, noise
10 pence, pancake
11 basket, bowl
12

```
B R A I N S
U   L   T
T O M A T O
T   O   R
O R N A T E
N   D   D
```

13

```
C R I N G E
O   M   O
U P P E R S
P   I   G
L E S S O N
E   H   N
```

14

```
P O R O U S
A   R   O
L E A D E R
A   E   E
C L E R K S
E   S   T
```

15

```
S U M M E R
P   O   R
R E S U M E
I   T   I
N   N   N
G E Y S E R
```

16 e   19 f
17 t   20 c
18 h

TEST 19: MIXED

1 fire	9 lesser, preferred
2 light	10 85475
3 mark	11 61354
4 hide	12 3122175
5 call	13 CAGED
6 scene, chapter	14 FADED
7 pack, flock	15 BADGE
8 bull, drake	16 gravy, roast

17 father, aunt   19 rugby, home
18 rocks, waves   20 chime, clock

TEST 20: MIXED

1 HAND	11 VALVE
2 OUT	12 25361
3 WOOD	13 86253
4 LIFE	14 53693
5 brake	15 CLAMP
6 set	16 WORMS
7 case	17 TURNS
8 tame	18 ZYQGL
9 pets	19 UHBDU
10 BALLET	20 QPPSW

TEST 21: MIXED

1 neglect, nurture	10 placid
2 trusting, wary	11 jumble
3 float, sink	12 cottage
4 many, few	13 soaked
5 PATH	14 prior
6 FLEW	15 Tq9,Nw6
7 FACT	16 JCE, JDI
8 SURE	17 LO, JQ
9 PRAY	18 jlm, rtu
	19 21Z, 5V
	20 QA, CW

TEST 22: MIXED

1 to, is	11 gasping, frail
2 the, his	12 are, prawns
3 led, stopped	13 split, wander
4 in, after	14 finer, thing
5 sky, air	15 8, 8
6 petrol, wheel	16 14, 20
7 find, weigh	17 1, 4
8 between, beyond	18 14, 20
9 pass, fail	19 12, 3
10 often, regular	20 10, 7

TEST 23: MIXED

1 9   4 1   12 BETTER
2 6   5 7   13 BERET
3 2   6 5   14 RENEW
7 neglect   15 LARDER
8 messy   16 SAFER
9 rested   17 y   19 n
10 unfriendly   18 r   20 h
11 dreadful

TEST 24: MIXED

1 DESIRE
2 DESERT
3 VERSE
4 RESIST
5 THROB
6 beat, drum
7 criticise, disapprove
8 essential, necessary
9 band, strip
10 17X, 5A
11 IJL, QRT
12 YVX, YWP
13 FU, DW
14 yDb, tSg
15 JPG, HOA
16 c
17 d
18 e
19 f
20 c

TEST 25: MIXED

1 l
2 r
3 f
4 t
5 RATE
6 NEST
7 BIRD
8 PASS
9 FLEA
10 EQCEJ
11 KXHMF
12 KNEAB
13 BALLS
14 THUMB
15 SALAD
16 crack
17 cover
18 concern
19 sweet
20 simple

TEST 26: MIXED

1 carpet, curtain
2 compress, evolve
3 shirt, trousers
4 balance, evenness
5 pole
6 hide
7 charge
8 swell
9 highly
10 EAR
11 HAS
12 ARM
13 PEA
14 RAG
15 Wednesday
16 Monday
17 31
18 28
19 59 years
20 1997

TEST 27: MIXED

1 moth
2 them
3 real
4 meat
5 rate
6 prize, appreciate
7 angle, viewpoint
8 cringe, squirm
9 crook, criminal
10 exit, outlet
11 plant, wiring
12 raid, stable
13 sink, trumps
14 hanged, witch
15 TRUST
16 STUDIES
17 STIFF
18 OPENS
19 ASHES
20 BRAVE

TEST 28: MIXED

1 JI
2 BY
3 OR
4 JQ
5 RS
6 TP
7 surround
8 vanish
9 inquisitive
10 perform
11 moveable
12 SLUMP
13 RESIGN
14 TOAST
15 RESPECT
16 SLIME
17 6pm, out, friends
18 gallery, variety, sculptures
19 brother, exam, party
20 eat, fruit, day

TEST 29: MIXED

1 WORDS
2 TROUT
3 JUICE
4 WATCH
5 SNOWS
6 blood, animal
7 lick, tongue
8 sentence, paragraph
9 ice, hail
10 8P
11 8J
12 8C
13 8Z
14 8A
15 8T
16 control, curb
17 tip, point
18 eagerness, zeal
19 lighten, reduce
20 aloof, distant

TEST 30: MIXED

1 b
2 w
3 s
4 p

5–8

9 7U, 5A
10 lf, Kg
11 UGG, TIH
12 RX, XA
13 NOG, LPI
14 EV, IR
15 15
16 24
17 26
18 12
19 18
20 23

TEST 31: MIXED

1 summit, base
2 torrent, trickle

3 truly, falsely
4 robust, sickly
5 peculiar, odd
6 note, observe
7 thrifty, frugal
8 perch, sit
9 swivel, turn
10 TALKS
11 CARDS
12 CLAIM
13 DIZZY
14 HAPPY
15 2nd April
16 10th April
17 4th June
18 5th July
19 C
20 C

TEST 32: MIXED

1 JANUARY
2 ICEBERG
3 TWICE
4 ENDED
5 BISCUITS
6 madden
7 critic
8 value
9 stifle
10 joint
11 WISH, FISH
12 GRIP, DRIP
13 GULL, GALL
14 PINE, PANE
15 13, 7
16 10, 8
17 5, 12
18 12, 16
19 11, 23
20 4, 32

TEST 33: MIXED

1-2 9th January
30th January
3-4 11, 48
5 50
6 08:28
7 08:45
8–11

12 @ 8 a ^ ?
13 t u p o
14 # ~ ! > /
15 a n s u r
16 ~ $ # ~ %
17 it
18 sh
19 ut
20 ap

TEST 34: MIXED

1 tense
2 fix
3 coast
4 weird
5 stay
6 gravel, tarmac
7 still, active
8 distant, far
9 compete, fight
10 SQ
11 QR
12 YX

13 KN   17 lit
14 WT   18 tone
15 KP   19 chat
16 witch   20 her

TEST 35: MIXED

1 FRAIL	11 SEVEN
2 PLEATED	12 FIGHT
3 CROUCH	13 EDDBK
4 PRIDE	14 IPMFT
5 shed	15 ECTTA
6 mean	16 flourish, thrive
7 scan	17 life, existence
8 vent	18 blank, clear
9 then	19 candid, frank
10 TABLE	20 signal, gesture

TEST 36: MIXED

1 start, conclude	12 hillock, mound
2 question, reply	
3 over, under	13 yap, bark
4 upright, reclined	14 swamp, marsh
5 2 8 18	15 FA, ID
6 10 9 70	16 3B, 9K
7 33	17 qF, mJ
10 entire, complete	18 IR, JQ
	19 GT4, UU2
11 part, split	20 BHO, DLM

TEST 37: MIXED

1 sick, nauseous	10 FILE
	11 HARM, HARP
2 ponder, contemplate	12 LAZE, LAME
3 paw, foot	13 REED, READ
4 depress, sadden	14 PEAT, MEAT
5 crime, offence	15 RQRRA
	16 GZTSJ
6 THIN	17 TIXET
7 STOP	18 CARRY
8 FAST	19 SMALL
9 PACE	20 SUGAR

TEST 38: MIXED

1 14, 19	4 10, 22
2 2, 6	5 4, 32
3 3, 9	6 4, 5

7 gate   13 flourish
8 bear   14 tetchy
9 also   15 hamper
10 tool   16 crowd
11 scar   17 be   19 el
12 clap   18 st   20 gn

TEST 39: MIXED

1 reed	10 BACK
2 net	11 KNEE
3 link	12 JERK
4 rot	13 SZOU
5 ten	14 DLIW
6 country, city	15 BZDM
7 skin, tooth	16 bold
8 brush, comb	17 sensible
	18 complex
9 estimate, outline	19 many
	20 fleeting

TEST 40: MIXED

1 PLANET	11 JSLAF
2 CASTLE	12 ZSCPX
3 BEACH	13 ZEBRA
4 FLATTER	14 BEANS
5 PASS	15 HUTCH
6 PORT	16 oak
7 HOLE	17 beech
8 LEND	18 maple
9 PAIR	19 ash
10 FZQCB	20 sycamore

Puzzle ❶

Leeds

London

Bristol

Puzzle ❷

WILD
LIFE **CAT**
BOAT GUARD **FISH**
MAN ROOM **EYE** FINGER
AGE DRILL **PIECE** BALL NAIL
SPAR OLD **WORK** ROOM POINT FILE
ROW RING **HORSE** PLACE FULL LESS FAN
WING LET **PLAY** FIELD MAT FILL STAR SING
BEAT **BACK** WORK MOUSE CUP UP GIRL
TEN **HAND** FORCE HOLE TIE GUARD
DON **SOME** NINE UP LINE
KEY **WHERE** TEEN EAR
AS FORE THEN
UNDER EVER
FOOT
WEAR BALL
OUT LOON **COCK**
WARD BOAT ATTIC **TAIL**
DEN GAME LOFT **GATE** OR
NOTE TASTE TEA **HOUSE** RANGE BIT
LET BLACK BUD **BOUND** TRAIN HEAVY TEN
HALL SPOT DING **LESS** NURSE LOAD DEER ANT
MARK ASK **ON** MAID DEAD SKIN THEM
KING **SET** LINE WEIGHT HEAD SELF
DOME **TEE** DANCE SHIP FISH
TOTAL **THE** FLOOR BONE
REIN **ME** PICK
DEER **AN**
GEL

Puzzle ❸

The treasure of Black Jack lies under the palm tree in the north of Dead Man's Island. X marks the spot. The X should be placed on the palm tree at the top of the map.

Puzzle ❹

G	R	O	W	S			E	A	G	E	R
R			O		N						A
I			R		R						N
N		E	R	R	O	R					G
S	U	N	N	Y			L	I	T	H	E
		T					F				
T	O	W	E	L			F	L	A	M	E
O			R	O	G	U	E				P
A			G		D						O
S			I		G						C
T	O	N	I	C			E	A	R	T	H

Puzzle ❺

LADY	EVENT	RELATIONSHIP	PLACE
Miss Millard	Tennis tournament	schoolchildren	Godalming
Miss Jones	Tea	Niece	Guildford
Mrs Pringle	Sunday lunch	Grandchildren	Surbiton
Mrs Prout	Nature ramble	Husband	Redhill
Mrs Snape	Swimming	Friend	Richmond

Test time: 0 |||||5|||||10 minutes

Rearrange the letters in capitals to make another word. The new word has something to do with the first two words.

Example: spot   soil   SAINT   ___STAIN___

1   wish, fancy   RESIDE   _____
2   abandon, leave   RESTED   _____
3   poem, lyric   SERVE   _____
4   endure, withstand   SISTER   _____
5   pulse, thump   BROTH   _____

Choose two words, one from each set of brackets, to complete the sentence in the best way.

Example: Smile is to happiness as (drink, <u>tear</u>, shout) is to (whisper, laugh, <u>sorrow</u>).

6   Blow is to trumpet as (call, beat, tap) is to (piano, drum, names).

7   Grumble is to complain as (speak, reply, criticise) is to (support, disapprove, encourage).

8   Require is to need as (essential, reject, consider) is to (necessary, hopeful, happy).

9   Belt is to strap as (group, musicians, band) is to (strip, flag, poster).

A B C D E F G H I J K L M N O P Q R S T U V W X Y Z

Give the missing letters and numbers in the following sequences. The alphabet has been written out to help you.

Example: CQ   DQ   EP   FP   <u>GO</u>   <u>HO</u>

10	____	5Y	17Z	____	17B	5C
11	ABD	EFH	____	MNP	____	UVX
12	XVZ	____	XVV	YWT	XWR	____
13	HS	GT	____	EV	____	CX
14	____	xGc	wJd	vMe	uPf	____
15	KOJ	____	IQD	____	GPX	FQU

If a = 5, b = 3, c = 10, d = 2, e = 20 and f = 4, find the value of the following calculations. Write your answer as a letter.

16   $(a^2 - e) \times d$ =   ____

17   $\dfrac{2e - bc}{a}$ =   ____

18   $\left(\dfrac{3c}{b}\right) \times d$ =   ____

19   $(4b - c) + d$ =   ____

20   $\dfrac{bc}{a} + f$ =   ____

25

Total ____

Which one letter can be added to the front of all these words to make new words?

Example: ____are ____at ____rate ____all _c_

1	____ever	____adder	____ease	____ink	____
2	____ant	____eel	____oast	____each	____
3	____rank	____lute	____able	____inch	____
4	____each	____race	____ouch	____win	____

Look at the first group of three words. The word in the middle has been made from the other two words. Complete the second group of three words in the same way, making a new word in the middle.

Example: PAIN INTO TOOK ALSO _SOON_ ONLY

5	PARK	PALE	LEFT	RAIL	_____	TERM
6	DUMB	DRAB	GRAM	NEWT	_____	DESK
7	BILE	BLUR	USER	BAIL	_____	RIND
8	BOND	FIND	FILL	FUSS	_____	PACT
9	RARE	REED	BEDS	FOOL	_____	DEAR

A B C D E F G H I J K L M N O P Q R S T U V W X Y Z

10 If the code for TRAINS is VTCKPU, what is the code for COACH? _____

11 If the code for HONEST is GNMDRS, what is the code for LYING? _____

12 If the code for HORSES is KNURHR, what is the code for HOBBY? _____

13 If the code for TENNIS is PAJJEO, what is XWHHO? _____

14 If the code for FINGER is DJLHCS, what is RISNZ? _____

15 If the code for CARROT is ZXOOLQ, what is PXIXA? _____

Underline the one word in the brackets which will go equally well with both the pairs of words outside the brackets.

Example: rush, attack cost, fee (price, hasten, strike, <u>charge</u>, money)

16 collapse, crumble cleft, crevice (hole, scratch, fall, fissure, crack)

17 cloak, screen insure, protect (underwrite, cover, lid, coat, conceal)

18 involve, affect worry, anxiety (unease, turn, effect, problem, concern)

19 pudding, dessert kind, pleasant (perfumed, good, smelly, sweet, adorable)

20 easy, effortless clear, plain (patterned, simple, natural, transparent, pure)

Total

TEST 26: **Mixed**

Complete the following sentences in the best way by choosing one word from each set of brackets.

Example: Tall is to (tree, <u>short</u>, colour) as narrow is to (thin, white, <u>wide</u>).

1 Floor is to (kitchen, carpet, ceiling) as window is to (curtain, pane, glass).

2 Compact is to (expand, compress, stretch) as develop is to (contract, shorten, evolve).

3 Button is to (chocolate, switch, shirt) as zip is to (leg, trousers, code).

4 Symmetry is to (balance, sides, shapes) as equality is to (inconsistency, evenness, irregularity).

Find a word that is similar to the word in capital letters and that rhymes with the second word.

Example: CABLE   tyre   ___wire___

5 STAFF   roll   _____   8 BULGE   bell   _____

6 CONCEAL   lied   _____   9 GREATLY   smiley   _____

7 RUSH   large   _____

Find the three-letter word which can be added to the letters in capitals to make a new word. The new word will complete the sentence sensibly.

Example: The cat sprang onto the MO.   ___USE___

10 The ace of HTS is a playing card.   _____

11 The dog CED the cat up a tree.   _____

12 The WTH from the fire filled the whole room.   _____

13 The magician made the rabbit APR from nowhere.   _____

14 Please don't ENCOUE him to misbehave.   _____

Matthew, Helen and Emma all have Music exams. Helen's exam is on Thursday 17th June. Matthew's exam is 8 days before Helen's and Emma's is 11 days after Helen's. On which days of the week do Matthew's and Emma's exams fall?

15 Matthew   _____   16 Emma   _____

Three generations of the Thomas family were born in 1935, 1966 and 1994.

17 How old was the grandfather when the father was born?   _____

18 How old was the father when his son was born?   _____

19 What is the age difference between the grandfather and the grandson?   _____

20 The grandson has a sister who is 3 years older. She was born in   _____?

(27)

Total _____

TEST 27: **Mixed**

Find the four-letter word hidden at the end of one word and the beginning of the next word. The order of the letters may not be changed.

Example: The children had bat<u>s and</u> balls. _____sand_____

1   Please help him otherwise we will be here for hours. _____

2   The horse rider crossed the main road carefully. _____

3   There always seems to be a problem. _____

4   Come quickly and meet me at the bus stop. _____

5   The caterpillar ate the cabbage leaf hungrily. _____

Underline the two words, one from each group, which are closest in meaning.

Example: (race, shop, <u>start</u>)   (finish, <u>begin</u>, end)

6   (winner, prize, valuable)   (appreciate, grow, extensive)

7   (angle, line, direction)   (triangle, viewpoint, degree)

8   (cringe, crimson, critic)   (subtle, squat, squirm)

9   (crutch, crook, stick)   (invalid, old man, criminal)

10   (door, entrance, exit)   (gate, outlet, fence)

Move one letter from the first word and add it to the second word to make two new words.

Example: hunt   sip   _____hut_____   _____snip_____

11   pliant   wring   _____   _____

12   braid   stale   _____   _____

13   stink   rumps   _____   _____

14   changed   with   _____   _____

A B C D E F G H I J K L M N O P Q R S T U V W X Y Z

15   If the code for DUSTER is 748310, decode 30483. _____

16   If the code for DUTIES is 135429, decode 9531429. _____

17   If the code for FIGHTS is o u a y e i, decode i e u o o. _____

18   If the code for SPOKEN is 8 4 ^ J Z ?, decode ^ 4 Z ? 8. _____

19   If the code for WASHES is U e 7 4 # 7, decode e 7 4 # 7. _____

20   If the code for VERBAL is / > £ 6 X !, decode 6 £ X / >. _____

Total [____]

Test time: 0 . . . . . 5 . . . . . 10 minutes

A B C D E F G H I J K L M N O P Q R S T U V W X Y Z

Fill in the missing letters. The alphabet has been written out to help you.

Example: AB is to CD as PQ is to RS

1	ZY is to SR as QP is to	___	**4**	BY is to EV as GT is to	___
2	EB is to AX as FC is to	___	**5**	FJ is to EF as SW is to	___
3	BC is to AD as PQ is to	___	**6**	KO is to KG as TX is to	___

Underline the word in brackets closest in meaning to the word in capitals.

Example: UNHAPPY   (unkind   death   laughter   <u>sad</u>   friendly)

7	ENVELOP	(letter	surround	packet	parcel	stamp)
8	DISAPPEAR	(emerge	materialise	appear	vanish	attend)
9	CURIOUS	(ordinary	crafty	inquisitive	careful	imaginative)
10	EXECUTE	(watch	perform	guard	scrutinise	search)
11	MOBILE	(stationary	static	motionless	inactive	moveable)

Rearrange the letters in capitals to make another word. The new word has something to do with the first two words.

Example: spot   soil   SAINT   ___STAIN___

12	slouch, sprawl	PLUMS	_____
13	leave, quit	SINGER	_____
14	pledge, salute	STOAT	_____
15	regard, admiration	SPECTRE	_____
16	sludge, ooze	MILES	_____

Complete the following sentences by selecting the most sensible word from each group of words given in the brackets. Underline the words selected.

Example: The (<u>children</u>, books, foxes) carried the (houses, <u>books</u>, steps) home from the (greengrocer, <u>library</u>, factory).

17   At (noon, 7 am, 6 pm) we are going (by, out, from) to supper with some (friends, homework, elephants).

18   The art (hospital, station, gallery) was filled with a wide (avenue, staircase, variety) of pictures and (sculptures, taxis, animals).

19   Neil's (brother, sister, grandfather) was busy revising for his (exam, holiday, school) so couldn't go to the (house, car, party).

20   Katie knows she should (eat, sleep, weigh) at least five portions of (bread, milk, fruit) and vegetables every (month, minute, day).

Total

A B C D E F G H I J K L M N O P Q R S T U V W X Y Z

1 If the code for SPEECH is VOHDFG, what is ZNUCV? _____

2 If the code for FISHED is DGQFCB, what is RPMSR? _____

3 If the code for ORANGE is KNWJCA, what is FQEYA? _____

4 If the code for LISTEN is OIVTHN, what is ZAWCK? _____

5 If the code for WINTER is YGPRGP, what is ULQUU? _____

Choose two words, one from each set of brackets, to complete the sentence in the best way.

Example: Smile is to happiness as (drink, <u>tear</u>, shout) is to (whisper, laugh, <u>sorrow</u>).

6 Sap is to tree as (skin, blood, water) is to (nose, animal, river).

7 Chew is to teeth as (walk, blink, lick) is to (tongue, nose, lips).

8 Letter is to word as (idea, punctuation, sentence) is to (chapter, paragraph, page).

9 Water is to rain as (fire, yellow, ice) is to (rainbow, hail, sunshine).

All six classrooms for Year 8 are on the same corridor.
Work out from the information below, which class has which room.

1		3		5

CORRIDOR

6	7	8		

Class 8P is directly opposite 8Z. Class 8A is between 8Z and 8T. Class 8C is not opposite another Year 8 class. Class 8J is in the middle of a row.

10 Room 1 _____   **13** Room 6 _____

11 Room 3 _____   **14** Room 7 _____

12 Room 5 _____   **15** Room 8 _____

Underline the pair of words most similar in meaning.

Example: come, go   <u>roam, wander</u>   fear, fare

16 control, curb   hold, carry   restrain, remain

17 tip, point   strange, normal   clever, idiotic

18 enthusiastic, indifferent   eagerness, zeal   grave, minor

19 lighten, reduce   bright, dark   relaxed, tense

20 smile, sneer   gracious, unkind   aloof, distant

30

Total

Test 30: **Mixed**

Which one letter can be added to the front of all these words to make new words?

Example: ____are   ____at   ____rate   ____all   *c*

1	____less	____east	____rake	____anger	____
2	____ash	____rite	____inter	____ailing	____
3	____park	____tripe	____have	____liver	____
4	____latter	____ink	____ray	____ending	____

Fill in the crosswords so that all the given words are included. You have been given one letter as a clue in each crossword.

5–8

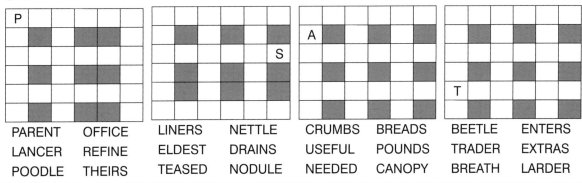

PARENT	OFFICE	LINERS	NETTLE	CRUMBS	BREADS	BEETLE	ENTERS
LANCER	REFINE	ELDEST	DRAINS	USEFUL	POUNDS	TRADER	EXTRAS
POODLE	THEIRS	TEASED	NODULE	NEEDED	CANOPY	BREATH	LARDER

A B C D E F G H I J K L M N O P Q R S T U V W X Y Z

Give the missing letters and numbers in the following sequences. The alphabet has been written out to help you.

Example: CQ   DQ   EP   FP   *GO*   *HO*

9	____	5W	7Y	____	7C	5E
10	Ab	Cc	Ed	Ge	____	____
11	WCE	VEF	____	____	SKI	RMJ
12	PW	____	TY	VZ	____	ZB
13	LOC	MOE	____	____	MPK	NPM
14	DW	____	FU	GT	HS	____

If A = 4, B = 9, E = 2, D = 6, R = 5 and S = 1, find the sum of the following words by adding their letters together.

15	DRESS	____	18	SEEDS	____
16	BREED	____	19	READS	____
17	BEARD	____	20	ADDER	____

Total [____]

Test 31: Mixed

Underline the two words, one from each group, which are the most opposite in meaning.

Example: (dawn, <u>early</u>, wake)   (<u>late</u>, stop, sunrise)

1   (summit, climb, success)   (base, top, ascent)
2   (torrent, river, waterfall)   (trickle, stream, flow)
3   (truly, quietly, thoughtfully)   (truthfully, absolutely, falsely)
4   (sink, robust, dive)   (submerge, swim, sickly)

Underline the two words, one from each group, which are closest in meaning.

Example: (race, shop, <u>start</u>)   (finish, <u>begin</u>, end)

5   (peculiar, subnormal, exact)   (odd, normal, ordinary)
6   (message, note, unseen)   (book, observe, buried)
7   (thrifty, few, elegant)   (numerous, extravagant, frugal)
8   (perch, fly, uphold)   (climb, sit, slide)
9   (effort, take, swivel)   (opportunity, turn, go)

A B C D E F G H I J K L M N O P Q R S T U V W X Y Z

10   If the code for SPEECH is TQFFDI, what is UBMLT?   _____
11   If the code for PACKET is RCEMGV, what is ECTFU?   _____
12   If the code for BOUGHT is ZMSEFR, what is AJYGK?   _____
13   If the code for AROUND is CTQWPF, what is FKBBA?   _____
14   If the code for SMILED is VLLKHC, what is KZSOB?   _____

The next Thursday after:

15   Thursday 26th March is _____
16   Thursday 3rd April is _____
17   Friday 29th May is _____
18   Saturday 30th June is _____

Read the first two statements. From the information, underline one of the options below that must be true.

19   Gill knocked on her friend's front door. No one answered so she went home.
   A Gill's friend was not home.
   B Gill's friend did not hear her knocking.
   C Gill was unable to visit her friend.
   D Gill's friend was unable to come to the door.

20   My garden has large trees. My garden has flowers which smell lovely when in bloom.
   A My garden doesn't have any grass.
   B My garden has more trees than flowers.
   C My garden has scented flowers.
   D My garden has trees under which flowers are planted.

Total

Test time: 0   5   10 minutes

Rearrange the muddled letters in capitals to make a proper word. The answer will complete the sentence sensibly.

Example: A BEZAR is an animal with stripes.   <u>ZEBRA</u>

1   NARAJYU is two months before March.   _____

2   The Titanic sank after hitting an BERCGEI.   _____

3   The dairy farmer milks his herd CITEW a day.   _____

4   The football match NEDDE in a draw.   _____

5   Would you like cheese and SCUBIITS or pudding?   _____

Underline the word in the brackets closest in meaning to the word in capitals.

Example: UNHAPPY   (unkind   death   laughter   <u>sad</u>   friendly)

6   ENRAGE   (enrich   relax   madden   soothe   calm)

7   DETRACTOR   (digger   critic   supporter   builder   follower)

8   APPRECIATE   (neglect   cost   value   approach   depreciate)

9   MUFFLE   (stifle   scarf   unwrap   sound   ruffle)

10   HINGE   (hanger   door   opening   gateway   joint)

Change the first word into the last word, by changing one letter at a time and making two new different words in the middle.

Example: TEAK   <u>TEAT</u>   <u>TENT</u>   RENT

11   WASH   _____   _____   FIST

12   GRID   _____   _____   DROP

13   GULP   _____   _____   GAOL

14   PINK   _____   _____   BANE

Give the two missing numbers in the following sequences.

Example: 2   4   6   <u>8</u>   <u>10</u>

15	16	15	___	11	10	___	7	3
16	14	13	11	___	___	7	5	4
17	2	3	___	8	___	17	23	30
18	9	10	___	13	15	___		
19	___	15	19	___	27	31		
20	2	___	8	16	___	64		

Total _____

Sharon's birthday is on 16th January. Mia's birthday is a week before Sharon's. Sara's birthday is two weeks after Sharon's.

1–2 What date is: Mia's birthday? _____ Sara's birthday? _____

Mrs. May was born in 1959 and had a son, Tim, when she was 29.

3–4 How old was: Tim in 1999? _____ Mrs. May in 2007? _____

5 How old will Mrs. May be when her son is 21? _____

A train leaves the local station at 07:30 and the journey to town takes 58 minutes.

6 At what time should the train arrive in town? _____

7 If the train is 17 minutes late, what time does it arrive in town? _____

Fill in the crosswords so that all the given words are included. You have been given one letter as a clue in each crossword.

8–11

WINTER	WILLOW
WOODEN	LATEST
TIERED	RETURN

IMAGES	EMERGE
SENSES	ESSAYS
EXISTS	ROGUES

KITTEN	TANNER
BASKET	BATTER
RUNNER	TARTAN

SCHEME	REDEEM
STORMS	TEMPER
RIOTER	SMOOTH

A B C D E F G H I J K L M N O P Q R S T U V W X Y Z

12 If the code for KINDER is $ 8 a @ ^ ?, what is the code for DINER? _____

13 If the code for AWAKEN is b x b l f o, what is the code for STOP? _____

14 If the code for SPRING is / > ~ ! ^ #, what is the code for GRIPS? _____

15 If the code for TRADER is a n u r s n, what is the code for TREAD? _____

16 If the code for SPONGE is % £ $ # ~ >, what is the code for GONGS? _____

Find two letters which will end the first word and start the second word. The same letters must be used for both pairs of words.

Example: rea (*ch*) air   tou (*ch*) oose

17 biscu (___) em   pla (___) alic   **19** sho (___) ter   ro (___) most

18 flu (___) ipping   wi (___) ower   **20** str (___) pear   he (___) ple

Total

Test time: 0   5   10 minutes

Find a word that is similar to the word in capital letters and that rhymes with the second word.

Example: CABLE   tyre   ___wire___

1   NERVOUS   fence   _____

2   ARRANGE   sticks   _____

3   SEASHORE   boast   _____

4   STRANGE   beard   _____

5   REMAIN   neigh   _____

Complete the following sentence in the best way by choosing one word from each set of brackets.

Example: Tall is to (tree, <u>short</u>, colour) as narrow is to (thin, white, <u>wide</u>).

6   Path is to (lane, gravel, way) as road is to (tarmac, cars, lines).

7   Stationary is to (paper, still, train) as movement is to (music, active, actor).

8   Near is to (last, next, distant) as close is to (shut, far, local).

9   Race is to (run, compete, win) as is to battle is to (fight, pursue, chase).

A B C D E F G H I J K L M N O P Q R S T U V W X Y Z

Fill in the missing letters. The alphabet has been written out to help you.

Example: AB is to CD as PQ is to RS

10   PN is to LJ as WU is to   ____   13   HI is to GJ as LM is to   ____

11   BE is to FG as MP is to   ____   14   QT is to QN as WZ is to   ____

12   BA is to ZY as AZ is to   ____   15   GT is to FU as LO is to   ____

Change the first word of the third pair in the same way as the other pairs to give a new word.

Example: bind, hind   bare, hare   but, ___hut___

16   patch, pitch   hatch, hitch   watch,   _____

17   site, tie   word, rod   silt,   _____

18   repatriate, tape   penalty, lane   cenotaph, _____

19   meaningful, meal   hinged, hind   chariot, _____

20   limestone, one   monkey, key   smother, _____

Total

TEST 35: Mixed

Add one letter to the word in capital letters to make a new word. The meaning of the new word is given in the clue.

Example: PLAN   simple   ___PLAIN___

1	RAIL	feeble	_____
2	PLATED	folded	_____
3	COUCH	bend	_____
4	RIDE	self-worth	_____

Find the four-letter word hidden at the end of one word and the beginning of the next word. The order of the letters may not be changed.

Example: The children had ba<u>ts and</u> balls.   ___sand___

5 She was so distraught, she dared not go in.   _____

6 Mr Patel drives home and parks the car in the garage.   _____

7 Those boys can be terribly annoying.   _____

8 All of us should succeed given time.   _____

9 The wind blew the newspaper across the park.   _____

A B C D E F G H I J K L M N O P Q R S T U V W X Y Z

10 If the code for NAPKIN is LBNLGO, what is RBZMC?   _____

11 If the code for TWELVE is RUCJTC, what is QCTCL?   _____

12 If the code for BATTLE is DZVSND, what is HHIGV?   _____

13 If the code for PEBBLE is SDEAOD, what is the code for BEACH?   _____

14 If the code for BUTTON is CVUUPO, what is the code for HOLES?   _____

15 If the code for BURDEN is DWTFGP, what is the code for CARRY?   _____

Underline the pair of words most similar in meaning.

Example: come, go   <u>roam, wander</u>   fear, fare

16	despair, destroy	succeed, fail	flourish, thrive
17	death, heaven	life, existence	dead, alive
18	blank, clear	empty, full	vacant, engaged
19	noisy, silent	candid, frank	vocal, vivid
20	front, side	half, whole	signal, gesture

Total _____

Underline the two words, one from each group, which are the most opposite in meaning.

Example: (dawn, <u>early</u>, wake)   (<u>late</u>, stop, sunrise)

1   (start, finish, leap)   (jump, conclude, walk)

2   (remorse, recur, question)   (reply, repent, repeat)

3   (beneath, over, beside)   (near, inside, under)

4   (slanted, upright, tilted)   (reclined, moving, rushing)

If p = 4, q = 7, r = 11, s = 3 and t = 12, find the value of the following calculations.

5 $\dfrac{st}{p} - q$ =   ____

6 $\dfrac{q + r + t}{s}$ =   ____

7 $q^2 - p^2$ =   ____

8 $(4q - 2r) \times s$ =   ____

9 $qr - (p + s)$ =   ____

Underline the two words, one from each group, which are closest in meaning.

Example: (race, shop, <u>start</u>)   (finish, <u>begin</u>, end)

10   (entire, constant, broken)   (complete, part, weary)

11   (part, top, attach)   (resume, split, pierce)

12   (hillock, mountain, cliff)   (pit, hole, mound)

13   (tree, yap, elephant)   (bark, leaf, trunk)

14   (swamp, fill, battle)   (march, swallow, marsh)

A B C D E F G H I J K L M N O P Q R S T U V W X Y Z

Give the missing letters and numbers in the following sequences. The alphabet has been written out to help you.

Example: CQ   DQ   EP   FP   <u>GO</u>   <u>HO</u>

15   DY   EZ   ____   GB   HC   ____

16   ____   5E   7H   ____   11N   13Q

17   sD   ____   oH   ____   kL   iN

18   HS   ____   ____   KP   LO   MN

19   GP64   UQ32   GR16   US8   ____   ____

20   ____   CJN   ____   ENL   FPK   GRJ

Total _____

Underline the pair of words most similar in meaning.

Example: come, go   <u>roam, wander</u>   fear, fare

1	sick, nauseous	enriched, impoverished	second-rate, first-class
2	think, mind	ponder, contemplate	brain, brawn
3	claw, beak	talon, limb	paw, foot
4	oppress, iron	depress, sadden	impress, ignore
5	crime, offence	penalty, kick	guilt, innocence

Look at the first group of three words. The word in the middle has been made from the other two words. Complete the second group of three words in the same way, making a new word in the middle.

Example: PAIN   INTO   TOOK   ALSO   <u>SOON</u>   ONLY

6	BITE	TEAM	ARMY	WITH	_____	IONS
7	CAMP	CAME	MESS	STIR	_____	OPEN
8	POND	POUR	URNS	FARM	_____	STOP
9	TORE	TIME	LIMP	PUCE	_____	FACT
10	NODE	DONE	BIND	LIFE	_____	FLAG

Change the first word into the last word, by changing one letter at a time and making two new different words in the middle.

Example: TEAK   <u>TEAT</u>   <u>TENT</u>   RENT

11	FARM	_____	_____	HASP
12	LAZY	_____	_____	LIME
13	DEED	_____	_____	ROAD
14	PEST	_____	_____	MEAN

A B C D E F G H I J K L M N O P Q R S T U V W X Y Z

15	If the code for ZINNIA is BKPPKC, what is the code for POPPY?	_____
16	If the code for PLANET is RKCMGS, what is the code for EARTH?	_____
17	If the code for STREAM is UTTECM, what is the code for RIVER?	_____
18	If the code for BASKET is ZYQICR, what is AYPPW?	_____
19	If the code for LITTLE is MJUUMF, what is TNBMM?	_____
20	If the code for SWEETS is UVGDVR, what is UTIZT?	_____

38

Total

Give the two missing numbers in the following sequences.

Example: 2   4   6   _8_   _10_

1	5	10	___	17	___	20		
2	3	___	___	4	9	6	12	8
3	___	4	6	7	___	10	12	13
4	7	___	13	16	19	___		
5	___	8	16	___	64	128		
6	4	1	4	3	___	___	4	7

Find the four-letter word hidden at the end of one word and the beginning of the next word. The order of the letters may not be changed.

Example: The children had ba<u>ts and</u> balls.   ___sand___

7   Marion's dog ate the cake.   _____

8   Members of that tribe are fierce.   _____

9   The bicycle wheel crushed the petals of a flower.   _____

10   My uncle is too large for his chair.   _____

11   His brother ran out of petrol in his car.   _____

Underline the word in the brackets closest in meaning to the word in capitals.

Example: UNHAPPY   (unkind   death   laughter   <u>sad</u>   friendly)

12   APPLAUD   (apply   clap   claim   arrival   constant)

13   PROSPER   (right   fail   view   chance   flourish)

14   SNAPPY   (twisty   chatty   tetchy   steal   smart)

15   HINDER   (behind   front   back   hamper   picnic)

16   HORDE   (crowd   divide   solo   alone   empty)

Find two letters which will end the first word and start the second word. The same letters must be used for both pairs of words.

Example: rea (_ch_) air   tou (_ch_) oose

17   ro   (___)   ast   tri   (___)   ater

18   bur   (___)   oop   wri   (___)   ump

19   cam   (___)   der   whe   (___)   ves

20   si   (___)   ome   rei   (___)   aw

Total

Change the first word of the third pair in the same way as the other pairs to give a new word.

Example: bind, hind   bare, hare   but, _____hut_____

1	dear, deer	pear, peer	read,	_____
2	lamp, map	pond, nod	went,	_____
3	current, rent	curate, rate	cufflink,	_____
4	limpid, dip	organ, nag	mentor,	_____
5	biscuit, bit	analogy, any	television,	_____

Complete the following sentence in the best way by choosing one word from each set of brackets.

Example: Tall is to (tree, <u>short</u>, colour) as narrow is to (thin, white, <u>wide</u>).

6   Rural is to (country, road, boundary) as urban is to (avenue, crowd, city).

7   Pore is to (spot, flow, skin) as cavity is to (hole, sore, tooth).

8   Bristle is to (brush, hedgehog, thistle) as tooth is to (fang, mouth, comb).

9   Gauge is to (inspect, estimate, purchase) as draft is to (military, outline, complete).

A B C D E F G H I J K L M N O P Q R S T U V W X Y Z
Using the code Z stands for A, Y for B, X for C and so on, decode these words:

| **10** | YZXP | _____ | **12** | QVIP | _____ |
| **11** | PMVV | _____ | | | |

Encode these words:

| **13** | HALF | _____ | **15** | YAWN | _____ |
| **14** | WORD | _____ | | | |

Underline the word in the brackets which is most opposite in meaning to the word in capitals.

Example: WIDE   (broad   vague   long   <u>narrow</u>   motorway)

16	TIMID	(nervous	shy	bashful	bold	meek)
17	IDIOTIC	(sensible	senseless	careless	thoughtless	edible)
18	SIMPLE	(comprehensible	plain	complex	complete	right)
19	SOLE	(laces	fish	body	single	many)
20	TIMELESS	(late	ageless	enduring	classic	fleeting)

Total

Test 40: **Mixed**

Test time: 0 ... 5 ... 10 minutes

Add one letter to the word in capital letters to make a new word. The meaning of the new word is given in the clue.

Example: PLAN   simple   ___PLAIN___

1   PLANT   celestial body   _____
2   CASTE   fortified building   _____
3   EACH   seashore   _____
4   LATTER   compliment   _____

Find the four-letter word which can be added to the letters in capitals to make a new word. The new word will complete the sentence sensibly.

Example: At the zoo, we visited the REP house.   ___TILE___

5   Take the COM with you when you go hiking.   _____
6   It is IMANT to take care crossing a road.   _____
7   A half added to a half makes one W.   _____
8   The queen looked SPID in her ceremonial robes.   _____
9   He was filled with DES when he saw the damage to his home.   _____

A B C D E F G H I J K L M N O P Q R S T U V W X Y Z

10   If the code for STRIPE is VSUHSD, what is the code for CANDY?   _____
11   If the code for DINNER is BGLLCP, what is the code for LUNCH?   _____
12   If the code for CASTLE is BBQVIH, what is the code for ARENA?   _____
13   If the code for AFRICA is CHTKEC, what is BGDTC?   _____
14   If the code for NINETY is LJLFRZ, what is ZFYOQ?   _____
15   If the code for RABBIT is PYZZGR, what is FSRAF?   _____

There are five trees at the bottom of my garden. Work out where each tree is planted.

↑ NORTH

A ●   B ●

C ●

D ●   E ●

The maple is more northerly than the sycamore but more southerly than the beech. The ash and the oak are west of the sycamore. The oak is northwest of the maple.

16   A   _____
17   B   _____
18   C   _____
19   D   _____
20   E   _____

41

Total

Puzzle ❶

City Search

Take one letter from the first word and place it in the second word so that two new words are formed. The order of the letters may not be changed. The first word has been done to help you.

Then, rearrange the letters you have removed to make a well-known city and write it on the line. A clue has been provided to help you.

pile	sea	_pie_	_seal_	_L_
share	beats	_____	_____	___
really	wrath	_____	_____	___
pine	grim	_____	_____	___
shrewd	read	_____	_____	___

CITY: _____ A Yorkshire university town.

snore	wide	_____	_____	___
mouse	fund	_____	_____	___
wander	wet	_____	_____	___
drink	rip	_____	_____	___
camel	east	_____	_____	___
boat	vary	_____	_____	___

CITY: _____ A capital choice.

bleak	sack	_____	_____	___
rain	sad	_____	_____	___
boar	pen	_____	_____	___
wring	pay	_____	_____	___
meant	rust	_____	_____	___
bred	tale	_____	_____	___
spear	flight	_____	_____	___

CITY: _____ A city in the west of England on the River Avon.

Puzzle ❷

Start at the top of the pile of bricks and, working through the layers, make new words by combining two words, one from one layer and the other from the layer below it.

You must go down each time, not sideways.

Here is an example:

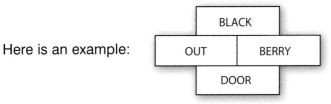

Both BLACKOUT and BLACKBERRY are new words, but only OUTDOOR makes sense as the next word.

Now try these. Be careful, there is only one path through!

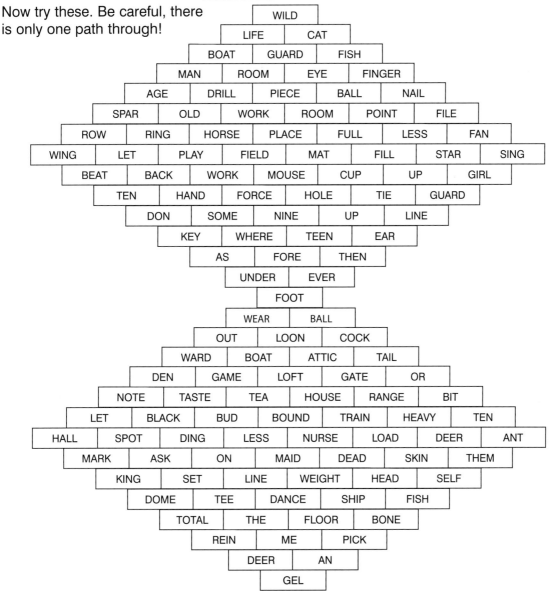

43

Puzzle ❸

Black Jack's Treasure

Here is a pirate's treasure map that is written partly in a letter code and partly in a picture code.

Work out what the information says, then place an X on the spot where the treasure is buried. The alphabet has been written out to help you.

A B C D E F G H I J K L M N O P Q R S T U V W X Y Z

Puzzle ④

Five Square Crossword

Put the words below into the crossword.

		O							
			Y						
		W			F				
									C

EAGER	EARTH	ENROL	ENTER	EPOCH
ERROR	FLAME	FUDGE	GRINS	GROWS
LITHE	LOGIC	RANGE	RIFLE	ROGUE
SORRY	SUNNY	TONIC	TOWEL	TOAST

Puzzle 5

Sunday Activities

Five ladies living in Surrey had good reason for wanting the weather to be fine the following Sunday.

From the information below and using the grid to help you, work out where each lady is going, what they are doing and who they are visiting.

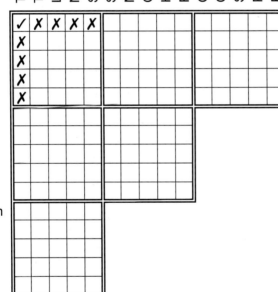

Miss Millard is organising a tennis tournament.

One of the ladies has a niece who lives in Guildford.

The grandchildren are having Sunday lunch in Surbiton.

Mrs Prout and her husband are not going out for a meal.

The countryside near Redhill is where the nature ramble is being planned.

Mrs Snape is visiting her friend's home in Richmond.

Miss Jones does not have grandchildren but she is going out to tea with her niece.

LADY	EVENT	RELATIONSHIP	PLACE
Miss Millard			
Miss Jones			
Mrs Pringle			
Mrs Prout			
Mrs Snape			

Progress Grid

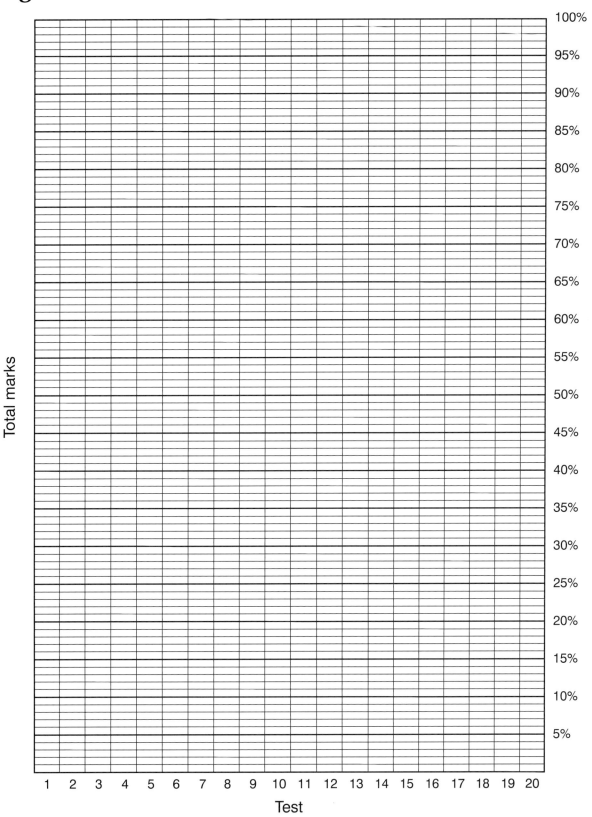

Total marks

100%
95%
90%
85%
80%
75%
70%
65%
60%
55%
50%
45%
40%
35%
30%
25%
20%
15%
10%
5%

1 2 3 4 5 6 7 8 9 10 11 12 13 14 15 16 17 18 19 20

Test

Progress Grid

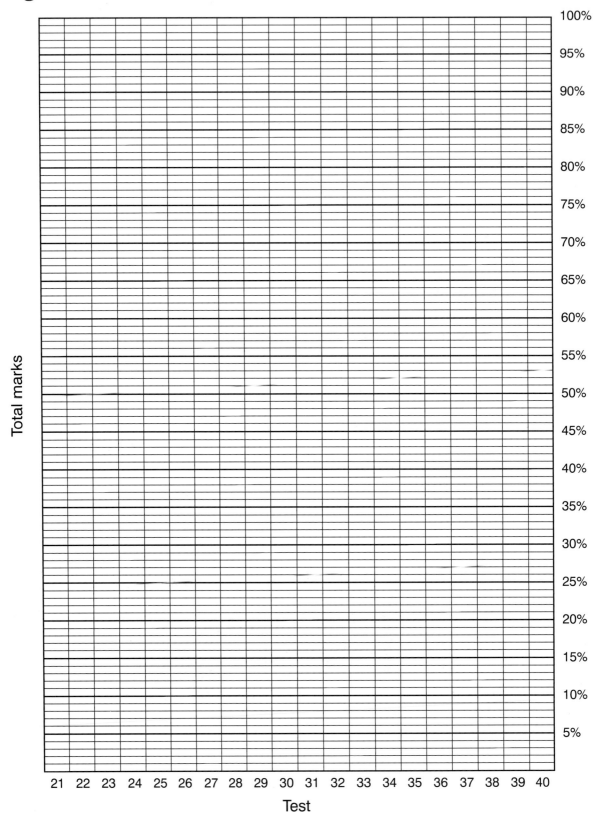

Total marks

100%
95%
90%
85%
80%
75%
70%
65%
60%
55%
50%
45%
40%
35%
30%
25%
20%
15%
10%
5%

21 22 23 24 25 26 27 28 29 30 31 32 33 34 35 36 37 38 39 40

Test